Cooking for Your Dog

Ingeborg Pils

Copyright © Parragon Books Ltd
Queen Street House, 4 Queen Street, Bath BA1 1 HE, UK

Produced by: ditter projektagentur GmbH
Project coordination: Michael Ditter
Food photography: Jo Kirchherr
Food styling: Rafael Pranschke
Dog photographs: Irmgard Elsner, Felix Sodomann (p. 1)
Illustrations: Kyra Stempell
Design: Sabine Vonderstein
US edition produced by: Cambridge Publishing
   Management Ltd
Translation: Susan James
Copy-editing: Sandra Stafford

ISBN: 978-1-4054-9514-1

Printed in China

Contents

Introduction

Cooking for your dog? If the very idea results in a frown of disbelief, you've never looked into the expectant eyes of a dog that has just noticed a human making his or her way to the kitchen. Of course, there is plenty of convenience food for our four-legged friends—cans with many different flavors and even more additives, health-store dried food made from organic ingredients, food recommended by veterinary surgeons worldwide, and a lot of rubbish packaged to attract human beings. But the same food day in, day out, the same flavor—that really does sound like a dog's life.

If you share your home and your daily life with a dog, and you like to cook, there will come a time when you won't be able to resist the temptation to cook something for your furry friend—either because you have rice or pasta left over, because it's a shame to throw meat trimmings into the trash, or just because Sammy, Susie, or Rover has earned a treat and a change from their everyday feed.

It's really very simple; dogs like many things that we eat too. Some things are taboo; processed food with chemical additives, highly spiced food, fat, salt, sugar, and chocolate should never end up in the dog bowl. Instead, use vegetables, fresh herbs, lean meat, fish, high-quality vegetable oils, yogurt, and other dairy products, and keep your dog happy and healthy.

These recipes are easy to cook and have been tried out by a whole pack of dogs—from dachshunds to Dalmatians—with plenty of enthusiasm and a hearty appetite. We have not given quantities for portions, because a dog's food depends on size, age, and mobility. Dogs that are fast on their feet need more nourishment than cuddly couch potatoes.

Cooking for dogs is fun for everyone. Just try it some time. Perhaps you'll feel as happy as I do when my crossbred bitch Gemma, after finishing her Gourmet Bowl, licks her chops and gazes at me contentedly.

The German actor and self-confessed dog-lover Heinz Rühmann (1902–1994), when asked if it were possible to live without a dog, answered, "Yes, but it's not worth it." This book is dedicated to him and all my four-legged friends.

Ingeborg Pils

TASTY TREATS
FOR
GOURMETS

PIPPA'S PASTA PLATE

5 oz (150 g) lamb
1 small clove of garlic
1 tablespoon olive oil
1 carrot
3½ oz (100 g) mushrooms
3½ oz (100 g) frozen peas
3½ oz (100 g) thin pasta for soup
1 tablespoon grated Swiss cheese (Emmental)

Dice the lamb into very small cubes. Peel and finely chop the garlic. Brown the meat and garlic in olive oil. Peel the carrot, grate, add to the meat, add ½ cup (125 ml) water, and simmer together for 15 minutes.

In the meantime, peel and chop the mushrooms. Add to the meat together with the defrosted peas and simmer for a further 5 minutes.

Cook the pasta in unsalted water till *al dente*. Drain and mix with the lamb and vegetable mixture. Allow to cool, sprinkle with cheese, and serve in portions.

SPRING VEGETABLE BOWL

$3\frac{1}{2}$ oz (100 g) new carrots
$3\frac{1}{2}$ oz (100 g) asparagus
$3\frac{1}{2}$ oz (100 g) cauliflower florets
$3\frac{1}{2}$ oz (100 g) scallions
1 clove garlic
1 tablespoon vegetable oil
$1\frac{1}{4}$ cups (300 ml) unsalted vegetable stock
$1\frac{1}{2}$ cups (150 g) porridge oats
1 tablespoon chopped spring herbs

Peel the vegetables and cut into small pieces. Finely chop the scallions and garlic. Heat the oil and sauté, then add the vegetable stock and simmer, covered, for 10 minutes on a medium heat. Add the porridge oats and cook for a few minutes. Take off the stove and allow to cool, then stir in the spring herbs.

Serve in portions, lukewarm or cold.

FISH À LA FIFI

7 oz (200 g) frozen fish fillet
1 cup (200 g) short-grain rice
   (pudding rice)
1 leek
1 hard-boiled egg
2 tomatoes, diced
1 tablespoon olive oil
a few leaves of basil

Defrost the fish fillet. Cook the rice with two cups of water until almost mushy. Remove from the stove.

Clean the leek, halve it lengthways, wash it thoroughly, and cut into very thin strips. Peel the egg and chop finely.

Fry the fish in olive oil on both sides. Add the leek and tomatoes, and fry together with the fish for another five minutes. Remove from the heat and break up the fish with a fork. Stir in the rice and the chopped egg. Cut the basil leaves into small strips and sprinkle over the food before feeding. Feed in portions.

"Give man a dog for
the health of his soul."

Hildegard von Bingen

Bella's Favorite Dish

2 onions
4 carrots
2 tablespoons (30 g) butter
7 oz (200 g) ground beef
1 tablespoon tomato paste
2 cups (500 ml) unsalted vegetable stock
5 oz (150 g) canned sweetcorn

Peel the onions and carrots, and dice into small cubes. Heat the butter and sauté the onions until transparent. Add the ground beef. Stir in the tomato paste, add the diced carrots, and pour on the vegetable stock. Simmer for 20 minutes.

Mix in the sweetcorn, bring to the boil, and remove from the heat. Allow to cool and feed in portions.

PAN-COOKED CHICKEN

1 zucchini
2 carrots
2 cloves garlic
4 potatoes
9 oz (250 g) chicken
1 apple
1 tablespoon oil
1 tablespoon finely chopped parsley

Dice the zucchini and carrots into small cubes. Peel and finely chop the garlic. Peel and dice the potatoes. Bring to the boil in $1\frac{1}{4}$ cups (300 ml) of water and simmer on a medium heat for 20 minutes. Then purée roughly in a food processor.

Dice the chicken and the apple into small cubes, and brown lightly in oil. Cook for 10 minutes on a low heat. Then mix with the puréed vegetables and stir in the parsley. Feed in portions, lukewarm or cold.

DELICIOUS
FOR ANY DOG

GOURME

BONNY'S FAVORITE PANCAKES

For the pancakes:
1 cup (120 g) whole wheat flour
2 eggs
1 cup (250 ml) skimmed milk
1 tablespoon finely chopped fresh herbs
vegetable oil for frying

For the filling:
5 oz (150 g) farmer's cheese
1 hard-boiled egg, chopped
1 puréed banana
5 oz (150 g) cooked rice

Mix the flour, eggs, and milk to make a batter and set aside for 20 minutes. Then stir in the chopped herbs.

In a frying pan with little oil, fry eight pancakes one after the other on a medium heat. Allow the pancakes to cool.

For the filling, mix the farmer's cheese with the chopped hard-boiled egg, the banana, and the rice. Spread the filling onto the pancakes and roll them up. Slice to feed.

The pancakes can be put individually into freezer bags, frozen, and defrosted as required.

BEEF CRUNCHIES

1 lb (500 g) lean beef

Dice the meat into half-inch (1 cm) cubes. Cover a baking sheet with baking parchment and place the cubes of meat on it, close together. Put into a cold oven and heat to 300°F (150°C). Cook the meat in the oven for 1 hour.

Reduce the oven temperature to 210°F (100°C), and prop open the oven door to allow the moisture to escape. Dry the cubes of meat in the oven for a further 2 hours.

Allow the beef crunchies to dry overnight at room temperature.

The crunchies will keep for up to a year in an airtight container—if your dog will allow it!

DEXTER'S DELIGHT

7 oz (200 g) beef
1 onion
1 clove garlic
7 oz (200 g) celery bulb
1 leek
2 carrots
2 tablespoons oil
1 cup (250 ml) unsalted chicken stock
7 oz (200 g) fish fillet
7 oz (200 g) cooked rice

Dice the beef into small cubes. Peel and chop the onion and garlic. Clean the celery bulb, leek, and carrots. Dice into small pieces. Heat the oil and brown the meat in it. Add the onion, garlic, celery, leek, and carrots, and sauté until translucent. Pour on the chicken stock, bring to the boil and simmer for 25 minutes.

Cut the fish fillet into small cubes and add it, with the rice, to the meat and vegetable mixture. Then remove from the heat and allow to cool. Feed in portions.

BILLY'S SPAGHETTI BOWL

9 oz (250 g) ground meat
2 tablespoons (30 g) fine porridge oats
1 egg
1 small onion
1 zucchini
½ bunch oregano
vegetable oil for frying
5 oz (150 g) cooked spaghetti
²⁄₅ cup (100 ml) organic tomato juice

Mix the ground meat with the porridge oats and the egg. Peel and finely chop the onion. Finely grate the zucchini. Strip the oregano leaves off the stalks and knead them into the meat mixture. Roll the mixture into little balls and fry slowly in a little oil until cooked.

Cut the spaghetti into small pieces and mix with the tomato juice.
Add the meatballs.

Feed in portions.

BANANA CHIPS

2²/₅ cups (370 g) whole wheat flour
²/₅ cup (100 ml) skimmed milk
1 egg
1 puréed banana
1 tablespoon corn syrup

Mix all the ingredients into a dough. Roll out the dough on a floured surface to ½ inch (1 cm) thickness and cut into small cubes. Preheat the oven to 300°F (150°C).

Cover a baking sheet with baking parchment and place the cookies on it. Bake in the hot oven for about 30 minutes.

VEGETABLE CRACKERS

1 zucchini
1 carrot
2 eggs
1 tablespoon sunflower oil
$1\frac{1}{4}$ cup (150 g) whole wheat flour
1–2 tablespoons milk

Grate the zucchini and carrot very finely. Mix with the eggs and sunflower oil. Knead in the flour and add enough milk to make an easy-to-shape dough.

Preheat the oven to 345°F (175°C).

Cover a baking sheet with baking parchment. Using a teaspoon, form the dough into little balls and place them on the baking sheet. Bake for 20–25 minutes in the hot oven. Then turn off the heat and allow the crackers to dry in the oven.

FOR BEST FRIENDS

GEMMA'S GOURMET BOWL

11 oz (300 g) lamb
2 tablespoons olive oil
4/5 cup (200 ml) unsalted chicken stock
2 sprigs rosemary
1 bay leaf
7 oz (200 g) Swiss chard
3½ oz (100 g) bean sprouts
2 beef tomatoes
11 oz (300 g) cooked rice
1 hard-boiled egg

Dice the lamb and brown gently in the hot olive oil. Pour on the chicken stock.
Add the rosemary and bay leaf, and simmer for 25 minutes. Then remove
the herbs.

Roughly chop the Swiss chard and bean sprouts. Chop the tomatoes into
small pieces. Add the vegetables and the rice to the lamb. Cook together
for 5 minutes. Take off the heat and allow to cool.

Peel the egg and chop roughly. Feed the Gourmet Bowl in portions, sprinkling
each portion with chopped egg beforehand.

FOR MAX:
VEGETABLE AND POTATO PIZZA

7 oz (200 g) potato dumpling mixture
oil for greasing
2 tomatoes
3½ oz (100 g) button mushrooms
2 oz (50 g) peas
1 can tuna fish in water or oil not brine
3½ oz (100 g) mozzarella cheese
1 small onion

Preheat the oven to 425°F (220°C).

Press the prepared potato dumpling mixture into a greased pizza dish and draw up the edges. Slice the tomatoes and button mushrooms, and place on the dumpling mixture. Add the peas and tuna fish. Dice the mozzarella cheese into small cubes, slice the onion, and spread both over the pizza.

Bake for about 30 minutes in the hot oven. Allow to cool and cut into bite-sized pieces. Feed in portions.

TIFFANY'S POWER BOWL

1 casserole chicken
1 tablespoon unsalted organic vegetable stock
$\frac{1}{2}$ celery bulb
1 yellow bell pepper
1 green bell pepper
1 lb (500 g) white cabbage
1 small can kidney beans
1 cup (100 g) coarse porridge oats
5 oz (150 g) tofu

Cut the casserole chicken into four pieces. Put in a pot, cover with water, and add the vegetable stock. Allow to simmer for 1 hour. Then remove the chicken from the stock. Bone and skin it, and cut the meat into bite-sized pieces.

Peel the celery bulb and clean. De-seed the bell peppers and dice. Cut the white cabbage into thin strips. Add to the pot with the stock and cook for 20 minutes.

Stir in the drained kidney beans, oats, and diced tofu. Cook for a few minutes. Remove from the heat and allow to cool. Feed in portions, lukewarm or cold.

"A dog can say more
with a quick wag of its tail
than many people who
talk for hours."

Attributed to Louis Armstrong

LULU'S FEAST

1 lb (500 g) beef heart
1 red onion
2 cloves garlic
9 oz (250 g) potatoes
9 oz (250 g) carrots
9 oz (250 g) Chinese leaf
3½ oz (100 g) leaf spinach

Dice the beef heart into small cubes. Peel and dice the onion, garlic, and potatoes. Roughly grate the carrots. Bring all of these to the boil in one quart (1 liter) of water and allow to simmer for 20 minutes.

Cut the Chinese leaf and spinach into small strips, and mix into the other ingredients. Cook for a further 10 minutes. Remove from heat and allow to cool. Feed in portions.

Classic Dog Cookies

3¾ cups (450 g) cups whole wheat flour
1¾ cups (170 g) porridge oats
2 tablespoons (30 g) shortening (pork lard)
1 tablespoon safflower oil
1 oz (40 g) grated Parmesan cheese
1¾ cups (400 ml) unsalted chicken stock
5 cloves garlic
3 carrots

Mix the flour, oats, shortening, oil, and Parmesan cheese thoroughly.
Add chicken stock and mix to a dough.

Preheat the oven to 320°F (160°C).

Peel the garlic and chop finely. Finely grate the carrots. Mix them into the
dough. Roll out the dough on a floured surface to a thickness of about ¼ inch
(5 mm). Cut with a sharp knife to make diamonds, triangles, or squares.

Cover a baking sheet with baking parchment and place the dog cookies on it.
Bake in the hot oven for 40–50 minutes. Turn off the heat and allow the
cookies to dry out in the oven.

LA DOLCE VITA—DOG-STYLE

Birthday Cake

1 lb (500 g) cooked floury potatoes
1 onion
3 tablespoons olive oil
1 lb (500 g) ground beef
3½ oz (100 g) raisins
3 hard-boiled eggs, peeled and chopped
1 bunch finely chopped parsley
3 eggs, beaten
2 tablespoons milk

1 teaspoon baking powder
2 tablespoons rye flour
1 tablespoon golden syrup
3 tablespoons (45 g) butter, softened
oil for greasing
4 tablespoons (60 g) grated Swiss
  cheese (Emmental)

Boil the potatoes in their skins. Peel them and press through a ricer while still warm. Store in a cool place.

Peel the onion and chop finely. Fry in the hot olive oil with the ground beef until the meat is crumbly. Mix in the raisins and the hard-boiled eggs. Remove from the heat.

Mix the riced potatoes with the parsley, eggs, milk, baking powder, rye flour, golden syrup, and butter.

Preheat the oven to 430°F (220°C).

Grease a cake pan. Fill with half of the potato dough and spread the ground beef mixture over the top. Spread the remaining potato dough on top and sprinkle with the cheese. Bake the cake for about 40 minutes in the hot oven.

Take out of the cake pan and place on a wire rack. Cool, then cut into pieces.

BENJI'S SNACKS FOR GUESTS

11 oz (300 g) sausage meat
11 oz (300 g) breadcrumbs
1 tablespoon golden syrup
⅓ cup (75 ml) milk
1 tablespoon chopped oregano leaves
oil for greasing
flour for dusting

Knead all the ingredients to make a soft dough. If the dough is too sticky, add more breadcrumbs. Shape the dough into a ball, wrap in plastic wrap, and allow to rest in the fridge for 20 minutes.

Preheat the oven to 345°F (175°C).

Grease six tartlet molds. Roll out the dough on a floured surface to about ¼ inch (5 mm) thickness, cut into circles, and place these in the tartlet molds. Bake in the hot oven for about 30 minutes. Remove from the molds, place on a wire rack, and allow to cool.

Bones for Special Days

1 cup (200 g) rye flour
1 cup (200 g) whole wheat flour
1 cup (200 g) wheat bran
1 cup (200 g) fine porridge oats
1 cup (250 ml) milk
1 tablespoon rapeseed oil
½ envelope dry yeast
2 tablespoons seaweed powder
flour for dusting
liver paté and farmer's cheese for the filling

Put all the ingredients except for the liver paté, farmer's cheese, and flour for dusting the work surface into a food processor. Knead to a firm dough. If necessary, add a little water. Place the dough into a bowl, put the bowl in a warm place and allow the dough to rise to double its volume.

Knead the dough thoroughly again and divide into four portions. On a floured work surface, shape each portion of dough into a roll and form the ends into bone shapes. The bones should be about equal in size and shape. Cover a baking sheet with baking parchment. Place the bones on the sheet, leaving a little space between them. Cover with a dish cloth and allow to rise for another hour.

Preheat the oven to 430°F (220°C).

Bake the bones in the hot oven for 20 minutes. Reduce the temperature to 320°F (160°C) and bake for a further 45 minutes. Then remove from the oven and allow to cool a little.

Halve the bones, while still hot, lengthways. Scoop out using a spoon. Place them hollowed-out side downwards and weight with a board so that they do not lose their shape when cooling.

To feed, fill one half with liver paté and one with farmer's cheese. Press firmly together.

Honey Dog Cookies

1¼ cups (150 g) whole wheat flour
1½ cups (150 g) porridge oats
2 teaspoons baking powder
2 tablespoons (30 g) butter
2 tablespoons honey
2 eggs
²⁄₅ cup (100 ml) milk
flour for dusting

Mix the flour, oats, and baking powder together thoroughly. Add the butter in small flakes, plus the honey, eggs, and milk. Knead together thoroughly.

Preheat the oven to 400°F (200°C). Cover a baking sheet with baking parchment.

Roll the dough out about ½ inch (1 cm) thick on a floured surface. Cut out round cookie shapes. Place these on the baking sheet, leaving some space between them, and bake in the hot oven for 15–20 minutes. Turn off the heat and allow the cookies to dry for a further 2 hours in the oven.

KEEP FIT AND HEALTHY

FRESH BREEZE

5 oz (150 g) coarse instant polenta
1 tablespoon maize oil
½ cup (125 ml) unsalted chicken stock
1 egg
1 tablespoon grated Parmesan cheese
2 tablespoons finely chopped mint

In a bowl, mix the polenta with the oil. Bring the chicken stock to the boil and stir in the polenta. Allow to thicken a few moments, stirring. Remove from the heat and cool.

Preheat the oven to 345°F (175°C). Cover a baking sheet with baking parchment.

Knead the remaining ingredients into the polenta. With wet hands, shape into walnut-sized balls and place these on the baking sheet. Bake for about 40 minutes in the hot oven. Turn off the heat and allow to dry for another hour in the oven.

FOR A GLOSSY COAT

1 apple
1 banana
2 carrots
2 cloves garlic
⅓ cup (100 ml) unsalted chicken stock
1 cup (200 g) porridge oats
1 tablespoon (30 g) diet margarine
1 tablespoon lecithin granules
1 hard-boiled egg
1 tablespoon finely chopped herbs

Purée the apple, banana, carrots, garlic, and chicken
stock in a blender. Then mix well with the oats, margarine,
and lecithin granules. Divide into portions.

Peel and roughly chop the egg.
Sprinkle each portion with the hard-boiled egg and the
finely chopped herbs when placed in the dog bowl.

WATCHING YOUR DOG'S WEIGHT

7 oz (200 g) lean beef
2 tablespoons safflower oil
11 oz (300 g) celery sticks
11 oz (300 g) fresh bean sprouts
7 oz (200 g) cooked bran
1 teaspoon vitamin and mineral mixture
3½ oz (100 g) low-fat yogurt

Cut the meat into small pieces and brown in a non-stick pan in the oil. Cut the celery into thin strips and add to the meat. Add a little water and simmer for 15 minutes.

Remove from the heat and allow to cool a little.

Roughly chop the bean sprouts. Mix the bran and sprouts with the meat. Divide into portions. When the portion is in the dog bowl, stir the vitamin and mineral mixture into the low-fat yogurt, and pour over the food.

COOKIES FOR HEALTHY TEETH

1¼ cups (150 g) whole wheat flour
1½ cups (150 g) wheat bread flour
1 cup (100 g) porridge oats
2 tablespoons (60 g) shortening (pork lard)
2 tablespoons rapeseed oil
3 tablespoons powdered skimmed milk
¾ cup (200 ml) unsalted chicken stock
flour for dusting
shelled sunflower seeds to coat

Mix the flour, porridge oats, shortening, rapeseed oil, and powdered milk thoroughly. Add the chicken stock and knead all the above to make an easy-to-shape dough. If necessary, add a little water.

Preheat the oven to 400°F (200°C).

Scoop out one tablespoon of dough at a time and shape a thick roll on a floured surface. Coat with the sunflower seeds.

Cover a baking sheet with baking parchment and place the cookies on it. Bake in the hot oven for 40–50 minutes. Turn off the heat and allow the dog cookies to harden for a few hours in the oven.

A CRUNCHY CURE FOR WIND

2½ cups (250 g) gluten-free flour (from health food stores)
1 egg
3 tablespoons olive oil
½ cup (125 ml) skimmed milk
1 teaspoon each finely chopped mint and parsley

Mix the flour, egg, olive oil, and milk to make a dough, not too firm, adding a little water or flour if necessary. Finally, mix in the chopped herbs.

Preheat the oven to 345°F (175°C). Cover a baking sheet with baking parchment.

Put portions of the dough into an icing bag with a star tip and squeeze out different shapes onto the baking sheet. Bake in the hot oven for 15–20 minutes. Turn off the heat and allow the dog cookies to dry for another hour in the oven.

WHEN YOUR DOG IS UNWELL

NOURISHING MASHED POTATO

11 oz (300 g) chicken breast
1 lb (500 g) potatoes
3½ oz (100 g) farmer's cheese

Cook the chicken breast for 20 minutes in a quart of water. Remove from the stock and allow to cool. Cut into small pieces.

Boil the potatoes in their skins in unsalted water until soft. Drain, peel, and make a soft mash with some of the chicken stock. Mix in the chicken and farmer's cheese. Serve at room temperature in several small portions throughout the day.

FOR CONVALESCENTS:

OATMEAL AND CHICKEN BOWL

1 casserole chicken
1 bunch mixed soup vegetables (1 carrot, 1 celery stick plus leaf, 1 leek, a little parsley)
1½ cups (150 g) fine porridge oats

Cook the chicken and mixed vegetables in 4 pints (2 liters) of water for about
1½ hours. Remove the vegetables and discard. Take the chicken out of the
stock and allow to cool a little. Skim and remove any fat from the stock.
Bone the chicken, remove the skin, and cut the meat into small pieces.

Stir the oats into 2 pints (1 liter) of the stock and bring to the boil.
Allow to thicken, stirring for 2 minutes, then remove from heat
and allow to cool.

Mix this thin porridge with the chicken meat in a 2:1 proportion
(⅔ porridge and ⅓ meat). Serve at room temperature in several
small portions throughout the day.

For Stomach and Digestion:
Rice Pudding Bowl

1 cup (200 g) short-grain rice (pudding rice)
3⅕ cups (750 ml) unsalted chicken stock
3½ oz (100 g) farmer's cheese or low-fat quark
1 apple

Cook the pudding rice in the chicken stock until soft. Then remove from the heat and allow to cool.

Stir the farmer's cheese or quark into the rice. Grate the unpeeled apple finely and stir into the rice mixture.

Serve in several small portions throughout the day, at room temperature.

TO HELP FIGHT CONSTIPATION:
DOG COOKIES WITH ALMOND BRAN

2 carrots
1 bunch parsley
¼ cup (60 ml) olive oil
1 lb (450 g) whole wheat flour
2 tablespoons almond bran
flour for dusting

Dice the carrots and roughly chop the parsley. Purée in a blender with the oil. Knead the purée, the flour, and the bran into a firm dough. If the dough is too dry, add a little water. Shape the dough into a ball, wrap in plastic wrap, and allow to rest for 30 minutes in the fridge.

Preheat the oven to 320°F (160°C). Cover a baking sheet with baking parchment.

Roll out the dough on a floured surface to a thickness of about ¼ inch (5 mm). Cut into shapes and place these on the baking sheet. Bake for about 30 minutes in the hot oven. Remove from the baking sheet, place on a wire rack, and allow to cool.